Family Prayers for Sleepyheads

Liguori
LIGUORI, MISSOURI

The Sleepyhead Bear children are tired and hungry. They have had a happy day playing in the garden and are waiting for Mommy Bear to finish cooking their dinner. While she is busy, Daddy Bear is going to read the children a story, to keep them out of her way.

"It's my turn to choose the story," cried Liz, the youngest Sleepyhead Bear.

"What have you chosen?" asked Daddy Bear, as he lifted her up onto his lap.

"It's called, FAMILY PRAYERS," said Liz.

"But that's not a story!" said Ben, her elder brother.

"I know!" cried Liz. "But it's my favorite book!"

"Then we shall read it," smiled Daddy Bear.

If you would like to read Liz's favorite book—then here it is!

Dear Lord,
Make the door of this house wide enough
To let in all who need love and kindness
And narrow enough to shut out
All quarrels, fights, and arguments.

Adapted from a poem by
Bishop Thomas Ken (1637-1711)

Lord, you know how busy I must be this day.
If I forget thee, do not forget me.

Sir Jacob Astley (1579-1652)

Help me to understand, Lord, that—
Little acts of kindness,
Little words of love,
Help to make earth happy
Like the heavens above.

Adapted from a hymn by Julia Carney
(1823-1908)

Lord Jesus, help me to remember...
He prays the best, who loves the best
All things both great and small;
For the dear God who loves us,
He made and loves us all.

Adapted from a poem by S.T.Coleridge (1772-1834)

Dear Lord, friend and brother,
of you three things I pray:
> To see you more clearly,
> Love you more dearly,
> Follow you more nearly,
> Day by day.

Richard of Chichester (1197-1253)

Let me be your child, Lord;
Where there is hatred, let me give love;
Where there is quarreling, friendship;
Where there is trouble, help;
Where there is crying, laughter;
And where there is sadness, joy.

Adapted from a prayer by St. Francis of Assisi
(1182-1226)

Thank you for the world so sweet,
Thank you for the food we eat,
Thank you for the birds that sing,
Thank you, Lord, for everything.

Traditional

Lord, your arms are stretching
Ever far and wide,
To cuddle close your children
To your loving side.

And I come, O Jesus:
I will not turn away,
For your love has called me,
And I come today,

Bringing all my worries,
Sorrow, sin, and care;
At your feet I lay them,
And I leave them there.

Adapted from a hymn by W. Walsham How
(1823-97)

Thank you, Lord, for...
All things bright and beautiful,
All creatures great and small,
All things wise and wonderful,
For you, Lord, made them all.

Each little flower that opens,
Each little bird that sings,
You made their glowing colors,
You made their tiny wings.

You gave us eyes to see them,
And lips that we might tell,
How great is God Almighty,
Who has made all things well.

Adapted form a hymn by Cecil Francis Alexander (1823-95)

God bless all those that I love;
God bless all those that love me.
God bless all those that love
those that I love,
And all those that love those
that love me.

New England Sampler

Dear God, be good to me;
The sea is so wide, and my boat
is so small.

Breton fisherman's prayer

Of what use is our restless, hurrying-scurrying?
For Lord, your way is clear,
And we, your little ones,
Need only one thing,
Trust in your love to meet our needs,
For only you, Lord, can take away all our cares.

Adapted from a prayer by Tukaram (1608-49)

Lord, teach me to love
your children everywhere,
because you are their Father and mine.

Anonymous

Bread is a lovely thing to eat—
God bless the barley and the wheat;
A lovely thing to breathe is air—
God bless the sunshine everywhere;
The earth's a lovely place to know—
God bless the folks that come and go!
Alive's a lovely thing to be—
Giver of life—we say—bless thee!

All good gifts around us
Are sent from heaven above;
Thank the Lord, O thank the Lord,
For all his love.

From a hymn by Matthias Claudius (1740-1815)

Lord, give your angels every day
Command to guide us on our way,
And bid them every evening keep
Their watch around us while we sleep.

So shall no wicked thing draw near,
To do us harm or cause us fear;
And we shall dwell, when life is past,
With angels round your throne at last.

From 'Around the throne of God'
by J.M.Neale (1818-66)